The Art of Building Relationships

Proven Strategies for Creating Strong Connections

Romeo B. Gross

All rights reserved. No part of this publication may be reproduced, distributed, or transmitted in any form or by any means, including photocopying, recording, or other electronic or mechanical methods, without the prior written permission of the publisher, except in the case of brief quotations embodied in critical reviews and certain other noncommercial uses permitted by copyright law.

Copyright © Romeo B. Gross, 2023.

Table Of Content

Chapter 1: Understanding the psychology of relationships

Chapter 2: Effective communication skills for building trust

Chapter 3: Setting boundaries and maintaining independence

Chapter 4: Navigating conflict and resolving disagreements

Chapter 5: Building emotional intimacy and vulnerability

Chapter 6: Creating shared goals and values in relationships

Chapter 7: Managing expectations and avoiding disappointment

Chapter 8: Maintaining a positive attitude and mindset

Chapter 1: Understanding the psychology of relationships

Understanding the psychology of relationships is a complex and multi-faceted subject that encompasses a wide range of theories and research findings. At its core, the study of relationships is concerned with understanding how and why people interact with each other, and how these interactions shape our thoughts, feelings, and behaviors.

One of the key psychological theories that informs our understanding of relationships is attachment theory. Developed by British psychologist John Bowlby in the 1950s, attachment theory posits that human beings have an innate need to form close emotional bonds with others, and that these bonds are critical to our survival and well-being. According to Bowlby, children form attachments to their primary caregivers, such as parents or grandparents, in order to ensure that they have a secure base from which to explore the world. As adults, we continue to seek out close relationships in order to feel safe and secure, and to have a sense of belonging and connection with others.

Another key theory that informs our understanding of relationships is social exchange theory. This theory, developed by George Homans in the 1950s, suggests that people engage in social interactions in order to gain rewards and avoid punishments. According to social exchange theory, individuals weigh the costs and benefits of a particular relationship, and will continue to engage in the relationship as long as the rewards outweigh the costs.

A related theory is the social exchange theory of close relationships, which suggests that people are more likely to form and maintain close relationships with those who are able to provide them with positive outcomes, such as emotional support, companionship, and intimacy. According to this theory, people are also more likely to end relationships that are not meeting their needs.

Another important perspective on relationships is the social cognitive theory, which focuses on how people learn to interact with others through observation and imitation. According to this theory, people learn about relationships by observing the interactions of others and then modeling their own behavior after what they have observed.

One of the most important findings in the psychology of relationships is the role of communication in relationship satisfaction. Research has consistently shown that effective communication is a key factor in maintaining healthy relationships. This includes both verbal and nonverbal communication, such as body language and tone of voice.

Another important area of research in the psychology of relationships is the study of love and attraction. Researchers have found that there are several key factors that influence the development of romantic attraction, including physical attraction, similarity, and familiarity. Additionally, research has shown that people who are in love tend to experience increased levels of dopamine and oxytocin, two chemicals in the brain that are associated with pleasure and bonding.

Perhaps one of the most important areas of research in the psychology of relationships is the study of conflict and its resolution. Researchers have found that conflict is an inevitable part of any relationship, and that how couples handle conflict can have a significant impact on the overall health of the relationship. Studies have shown that couples who are able to effectively communicate and compromise during conflicts are more likely to have satisfying and long-lasting relationships.

In conclusion, the psychology of relationships is a complex and multi-faceted field that encompasses a wide range of theories and research findings. From attachment theory to social exchange theory, social cognitive theory to the study of communication, love, and attraction, researchers have been able to gain a deeper understanding of how and why people interact with each other. Additionally, research has shown that effective communication, compromise, and the ability to handle conflict are key factors in maintaining healthy and satisfying relationships. It's important to understand that all relationships are unique, and that what works for one couple may not work for another. Therefore, it's important to be aware of these theories and findings and apply them in context to understand one's own relationships.

Short story base on experience:

I always thought I knew everything there was to know about relationships. I mean, I had been in a few of them and they all seemed pretty straightforward to me. But then, I took a class on the psychology of relationships and my whole perspective changed.

I learned about attachment theory and how our early childhood experiences shape the way we form and maintain relationships as adults. It made me realize that my fear of commitment and tendency to push people away was rooted in my own insecure attachment style, formed during my childhood.

I also learned about social exchange theory and how we weigh the costs and benefits of a relationship. I realized that in my past relationships, I had been too focused on what I could get out of them, instead of what I could give.

But the most eye-opening part of the class was learning about communication and how crucial it is in any relationship. I had always thought that as long as I loved someone, everything else would fall into place. But I realized that without effective communication, love alone is not enough.

So, I decided to put what I learned into practice in my current relationship. I worked on building a secure attachment with my partner, focusing on giving instead of taking, and constantly improving our communication. And it's made all the difference.

Our relationship is stronger and healthier than it's ever been. I never thought that understanding the psychology of relationships could have such a profound impact on my own life. But it just goes to show that knowledge truly is power.

Chapter 2: Effective communication skills for building trust

Effective communication skills are essential for building trust in any relationship, whether it be in a personal or professional setting. Trust is the foundation of all successful relationships and can be defined as the belief in the reliability, truth, ability, or strength of someone or something. Without trust, relationships can become strained and may ultimately fail. In this article, we will discuss some of the key elements of effective communication and how they can be used to build trust.

The first element of effective communication is active listening. Active listening is the process of fully focusing on and understanding the message being conveyed by the speaker. It involves paying attention to both verbal and nonverbal cues, such as body language and tone of voice. When communicating with someone, it is important to give them your full attention and avoid interrupting or dismissing their thoughts and feelings. By actively listening, you can show the other person that you value their input and are genuinely interested in what they have to say.

Another important element of effective communication is being transparent and honest. Transparency and honesty are essential for building trust because they demonstrate that you have nothing to hide and are open to being held accountable for your actions. When communicating with others, it is important to be honest and upfront about your intentions and actions. This will help to build trust and ensure that everyone is on the same page.

The third element of effective communication is empathy. Empathy is the ability to understand and share the feelings of others. When communicating with someone, it is important to put yourself in their shoes and try to understand their perspective. This can help to build trust by showing the other person that you care about their feelings and are willing to work together to find a solution.

The fourth element of effective communication is feedback. Feedback is the process of providing information to someone about their performance or behavior. It is important to give feedback in a constructive and positive manner. Giving feedback in a way that is critical or negative can damage trust and hinder the relationship. When giving feedback, it is important to focus on the behavior or action, rather than the person.

The fifth element of effective communication is effective use of language. Language is a powerful tool for building trust because it can be used to express oneself clearly and effectively. When communicating with others, it is important to use appropriate language that is clear, concise, and easy to understand. This will help to ensure that the message is received and understood as intended.

In conclusion, effective communication skills are essential for building trust in any relationship. By actively listening, being transparent and honest, practicing empathy, giving feedback constructively, and using appropriate language, we can build trust and strengthen our relationships. Remember, trust is the foundation of all successful relationships, and it takes time, effort and patience to build it. But when you do, the rewards are well worth it.

Here is a guide for effective communication skills for building trust:

- Be clear and concise in your communication. State your message in a way that is easy for the other person to understand.

- Listen actively. Show that you are paying attention and understanding the other person's perspective.

- Show empathy. Put yourself in the other person's shoes and try to understand their feelings and needs.

- Be honest and transparent. Be open and honest about your own thoughts and feelings, and avoid being manipulative or deceitful.

- Avoid making assumptions. Ask questions to clarify any misunderstandings and make sure you have a clear understanding of the situation.

- Be open to feedback. Be willing to listen and consider the other person's point of view, even if it differs from your own.

- Show respect. Treat the other person with dignity and respect, and avoid speaking in a condescending or dismissive tone.

- Take responsibility. Own up to your mistakes and apologize when appropriate.

- Follow through on your commitments. Keep your promises and do what you say you will do.

- Show gratitude. Express appreciation and thank the other person for their time and contributions.

By following these guidelines, you can develop effective communication skills that will help you build trust with others.

Chapter 3: Setting boundaries and maintaining independence

Setting boundaries and maintaining independence in a relationship is essential for creating a healthy and balanced partnership. A boundary is a limit or a line that separates what is acceptable and not acceptable behavior in a relationship. It is important to set boundaries in order to ensure that both parties in the relationship feel respected and valued. Maintaining independence, on the other hand, is about preserving one's individuality and maintaining a sense of self within the relationship.

One of the most important aspects of setting boundaries is communication. It is important to communicate with your partner about what you are comfortable with and what you are not. This can include things like how much time you spend together, how often you communicate, and what types of physical or emotional intimacy are acceptable. By clearly communicating your boundaries, you can avoid misunderstandings and prevent potential conflicts.

Another important aspect of setting boundaries is being assertive. Assertiveness is the ability to express one's needs and wants in a clear and direct manner. It is important to be assertive when setting boundaries because it shows that you are confident and secure in your needs and wants. Being assertive also helps to prevent others from taking advantage of you or crossing your boundaries.

In addition to setting boundaries, it is important to maintain independence in a relationship. Maintaining independence means preserving your own identity and individuality, rather than losing yourself in the relationship. This can include things like maintaining your own interests and hobbies, spending time with friends and family, and pursuing your own career or educational goals.

One way to maintain independence in a relationship is by setting aside time for yourself. This can include things like scheduling regular alone time or taking a class or hobby that you enjoy. By taking time for yourself, you can recharge and come back to the relationship refreshed and energized.

Another way to maintain independence in a relationship is by being open and honest with your partner. Being honest about your feelings and needs can help to ensure that both parties in the relationship are on the same page. This can include things like expressing your need for alone time or discussing your aspirations for the future.

In conclusion, setting boundaries and maintaining independence in a relationship is essential for creating a healthy and balanced partnership. By communicating your boundaries, being assertive, setting aside time for yourself, and being open and honest with your partner, you can maintain a sense of self and respect within the relationship. Remember that a healthy relationship is built on mutual respect, trust, and communication. By setting boundaries and maintaining independence, you can create a relationship that is fulfilling and satisfying for both parties involved.

Setting boundaries and maintaining independence in a relationship can feel empowering and necessary for maintaining a healthy balance in the relationship. It allows individuals to maintain their own sense of self while also respecting and valuing the needs and boundaries of their partner. It can also help to prevent feelings of resentment or being taken for granted.

However, it can also be challenging to navigate and communicate these boundaries and needs to a partner, and may require ongoing effort and open communication to maintain.

Advantages of Setting boundaries and maintaining independence in relationships

Setting boundaries and maintaining independence in relationships can have several advantages, such as:

- Maintaining a sense of self: Setting boundaries allows individuals to maintain their own values, beliefs, and needs, which can help them to feel more confident and self-assured in the relationship.

- Improving communication: By clearly communicating boundaries and needs, individuals can foster open and honest communication, which can lead to a deeper understanding and connection between partners.

- Building respect: When boundaries are respected and valued, it can lead to increased mutual respect and trust within the relationship.

- Encouraging personal growth: Having independence within a relationship can allow individuals to pursue their own interests, passions, and goals, which can lead to personal growth and fulfillment.

- Reducing resentment: When individuals feel that their boundaries and needs are not being met, it can lead to feelings of resentment. By setting boundaries and maintaining independence, individuals can reduce the likelihood of these negative feelings.

- Creating a healthy balance: Setting boundaries and maintaining independence can help to create a healthy balance within the relationship, where each partner feels fulfilled and respected.

Disadvantages of Setting boundaries and maintaining independence in relationships

Setting boundaries and maintaining independence in relationships can have some potential disadvantages, such as:

- Difficulty communicating: Clearly communicating boundaries and needs can be challenging, and may require ongoing effort and open communication to maintain.

- Potential for conflict: Setting boundaries may also lead to disagreements or conflicts with a partner, especially if there is a lack of understanding or communication.

- Risk of isolation: Maintaining too much independence within a relationship can lead to feelings of isolation or disconnection from a partner.

- Fear of rejection: Some individuals may be hesitant to set boundaries or maintain their independence due to fear of rejection or damaging the relationship.

- Fear of being alone: Some people may be hesitant to set boundaries or maintain independence because they are afraid of being alone, which can lead to compromise on personal values, beliefs, and needs.

- Fear of misunderstanding: some people may worry that their boundaries and independence may be misunderstood or misinterpreted by their partner, this can lead to confusion and mistrust.

It's important to note that setting boundaries and maintaining independence in relationships is not always easy, but it can be beneficial for both partners in the long run. It may require open communication, mutual respect, and willingness to compromise in order to find a balance that works for both parties.

How to manage the pressure in Setting boundaries and maintaining independence in relationships

Managing the pressure of setting boundaries and maintaining independence in relationships can be challenging, but there are some strategies that may help:

- Communicate clearly: Clearly communicate your boundaries and needs to your partner. This can help to avoid misunderstandings and ensure that your partner knows what you expect in the relationship.

- Be assertive: Stand up for yourself and your boundaries. It's important to be firm and assertive when communicating your needs and boundaries to your partner.

- Prioritize self-care: Take care of yourself and make sure you are not neglecting your own needs and wants. This can help you to feel more confident and empowered when setting boundaries.

- Seek support: Talk to a trusted friend or professional about your feelings and concerns. They can provide you with support and help you to see the situation from a different perspective.

- Be willing to compromise: Setting boundaries is not always easy and can sometimes cause conflicts, be willing to compromise and find a middle ground with your partner.

- Reflect on the reason of setting boundaries: Reflect on the reason why you are setting the boundaries and remind yourself of the long-term benefits it will bring to you and the relationship.

- Seek counseling if needed: If you find it difficult to manage the pressure of setting boundaries and maintaining independence, consider seeking couples counseling or therapy to work through any issues together.

It's important to remember that setting boundaries and maintaining independence is a process that may take time, and it may require ongoing effort and open communication to maintain a healthy balance in the relationship.

Chapter 4: Navigating conflict and resolving disagreements

Navigating conflict and resolving disagreements is an important skill to have in any setting, whether it be in personal relationships or in the workplace. When conflicts arise, it is important to approach the situation with a clear and open mind in order to find a solution that is acceptable to all parties involved.

One effective way to navigate conflict is to clearly define the problem at hand. This can be done by identifying the specific issues that are causing the disagreement and separating them from any personal feelings or emotions. Once the problem has been clearly defined, it is important to actively listen to the perspectives of all parties involved. This can be done by asking open-ended questions and repeating back what has been said in order to ensure that everyone's point of view is understood.

Another effective strategy for resolving disagreements is to brainstorm potential solutions. This can be done by creating a list of possible options and evaluating each one based on their potential impact and feasibility. It is also important to consider the interests and needs of all parties involved in order to find a solution that is fair and equitable.

Another effective technique is to use "I" statements. This method helps individuals to express their own feelings, thoughts and perspectives without blaming others or making them defensive. For example, instead of saying "You're always so stubborn" say "I feel frustrated when we disagree and can't find a solution."

It is also important to remain flexible and open to compromise. This can be difficult, but it is essential in order to find a solution that is acceptable to all parties involved. Remember, conflicts can be resolved in a way that benefits everyone.

Finally, it is important to follow up on the agreement reached. This can be done by setting a time and date to follow up on the progress of the solution, and to make any necessary adjustments.

In conclusion, conflicts and disagreements are a natural part of life. By clearly defining the problem, actively listening, brainstorming potential solutions, using "I" statements, remaining flexible and open to compromise and following up on agreements, conflicts can be resolved in a fair and equitable manner.

How Navigating conflict and resolving disagreements can influence relationships emotionally

Navigating conflict and resolving disagreements can have a significant impact on the emotional well-being of individuals and the overall health of a relationship. When conflicts are not effectively managed, they can lead to feelings of frustration, anger, and resentment. These negative emotions can damage trust and communication, leading to further conflicts and potentially causing a breakdown in the relationship.

On the other hand, when conflicts are effectively managed and resolved, it can lead to stronger, more resilient relationships. When individuals feel heard and understood, and when solutions are found that are fair and equitable, it can lead to an increase in trust and understanding between the parties involved. This can also lead to improved communication and an overall sense of emotional well-being.

Additionally, when conflicts are handled in a healthy and constructive manner, it can serve as a model for how to handle future conflicts. This can lead to an overall improvement in the emotional dynamics of the relationship, as individuals learn to effectively manage and resolve conflicts in a way that is beneficial for everyone involved.

Furthermore, when conflicts are resolved in a healthy way, it can lead to emotional intimacy and emotional bonding between the parties involved. This is because the act of working through conflicts together, and finding solutions that are acceptable to all parties, can create a sense of shared accomplishment and mutual understanding that can strengthen the emotional connection between individuals.

In conclusion, effectively navigating conflict and resolving disagreements is essential for maintaining healthy relationships. When conflicts are managed in a constructive and healthy manner, it can lead to an overall improvement in the emotional well-being of individuals and the emotional health of the relationship.

Can Navigating conflict and resolving disagreements have a negative impact in a relationship?

While effective conflict management and resolution can have a positive impact on a relationship, it is important to note that navigating conflict and resolving disagreements can also have a negative impact in a relationship if not handled properly.

One potential negative outcome of poorly managed conflicts is that they can escalate and lead to further disagreements and deeper resentment. This can cause a breakdown in communication and trust, leading to a negative impact on the overall health of the relationship.

Another potential negative outcome is that one or both parties may feel unheard or unimportant in the resolution process. If one person's perspective or needs are not considered, it can lead to feelings of frustration and resentment, which can damage the relationship over time.

Additionally, if conflicts are resolved through compromise, but the compromise is not fair or equitable, it can lead to one person feeling resentful or taken advantage of. This can also have a negative impact on the relationship.

Also, when conflicts are resolved by avoiding them or sweeping them under the rug, it can create a false sense of security in the relationship, and can lead to the conflict resurfacing in the future in a more intense form.

In conclusion, while effective conflict management and resolution can have a positive impact on a relationship, it is important to note that navigating conflict and resolving disagreements can also have a negative impact if not handled properly. It is important to approach conflicts with a clear and open mind, actively listen to all perspectives, consider the interests and needs of all parties involved, and find a solution that is fair and equitable for everyone. It's also important to communicate openly and honestly, in order to avoid any possible negative outcome.

Navigating conflict and resolving disagreements in relationships can be challenging, but with the right tools and approach, it is possible to effectively manage conflicts and build stronger, more resilient relationships. Here is a guide on how to navigate conflict and resolve disagreements in relationships:

- Define the problem: Clearly identify the specific issues that are causing the disagreement and separate them from any personal feelings or emotions. This will make it easier to focus on finding a solution.

- Listen actively: Actively listen to the perspectives of all parties involved. Ask open-ended questions and repeat back what has been said to ensure that everyone's point of view is understood.

- Brainstorm solutions: Create a list of potential solutions and evaluate each one based on their potential impact and feasibility. Consider the interests and needs of all parties involved in order to find a solution that is fair and equitable.

- Use "I" statements: Express your own feelings, thoughts and perspectives without blaming others or making them defensive. For example, instead of saying "You're always so stubborn" say "I feel frustrated when we disagree and can't find a solution."

- Be flexible and open to compromise: Remember that conflicts can be resolved in a way that benefits everyone. Be willing to compromise in order to find a solution that is acceptable to all parties involved.

- Communicate openly and honestly: Share your thoughts and feelings in an open and honest manner, and be prepared to listen to the thoughts and feelings of your partner.

- Follow up: Set a time and date to follow up on the progress of the solution and to make any necessary adjustments. This will ensure that the agreement is being upheld and that any issues are addressed in a timely manner.

- Seek outside help if necessary: If conflicts continue to arise and cannot be resolved on your own, consider seeking outside help from a therapist or counselor to help improve communication and understanding within the relationship.

In conclusion, navigating conflict and resolving disagreements in relationships can be challenging but with the right tools and approach, it is possible to effectively manage conflicts and build stronger, more resilient relationships. Clear communication, active listening, and a willingness to compromise are key in resolving conflicts and maintaining a healthy relationship. Remember, conflicts are normal, and it's important to approach them with a clear and open mind, and to find a solution that is acceptable to all parties involved.

Chapter 5: Building emotional intimacy and vulnerability

Emotional intimacy and vulnerability are essential components of any close relationship. They allow us to connect with others on a deeper level, share our thoughts and feelings, and build trust. However, building emotional intimacy and vulnerability can be challenging, especially if you haven't had much experience with it. Here are some tips for building emotional intimacy and vulnerability in your relationships.

Communicate openly and honestly. One of the most important things you can do to build emotional intimacy and vulnerability is to communicate openly and honestly with your partner. Share your thoughts and feelings, even if they may be difficult to express. Be willing to listen to your partner's thoughts and feelings as well.

Be vulnerable. Vulnerability is the foundation of emotional intimacy. It means being willing to share your deepest thoughts and feelings with your partner, even if you are afraid of being judged or rejected. Vulnerability allows you to connect with your partner on a deeper level and can lead to greater trust and intimacy in your relationship.

Practice active listening. Active listening is a powerful tool for building emotional intimacy. It means truly listening to your partner without interrupting or judging. When your partner is speaking, give them your full attention and try to understand their perspective. This can help you build trust and intimacy in your relationship.

Show empathy. Empathy is the ability to understand and share the feelings of another person. Showing empathy is a crucial part of building emotional intimacy and vulnerability. When your partner is going through a difficult time, try to understand their feelings and offer support.

Share your values. Sharing your values with your partner is another important aspect of building emotional intimacy. When you know what your partner values, you can understand them better and build trust and intimacy in your relationship.

Building emotional intimacy and vulnerability takes time and effort. It may be difficult at times, but the rewards are well worth it. Remember to communicate openly and honestly, be vulnerable, practice active listening, show empathy and share your values with your partner. With these tips, you can build a deeper and more meaningful relationship.

Short story experience

I met Sarah at a friend's party. We were both shy, and we didn't talk much that night. But something about her caught my attention, and I couldn't stop thinking about her. A few days later, I asked her out on a date, and she said yes.

At first, our relationship was easy and light-hearted. We would go out on dates, laugh, and have fun. But I soon realized that I wanted more. I wanted to connect with her on a deeper level, to share my thoughts and feelings, and to build trust. But I didn't know how to do that.

One day, I decided to take a risk and be vulnerable. I told Sarah about my fear of rejection, and how it had affected me in the past. I was surprised by how understanding and supportive she was. She shared her own fears and insecurities with me and we both felt like a weight was lifted off our shoulders.

From that moment on, our relationship changed. We started to communicate more openly and honestly. We listened to each other's thoughts and feelings and showed empathy. We shared our values, and our relationship became deeper and more meaningful.

As the days passed, we both became more and more comfortable in being vulnerable with each other. I shared my deepest thoughts and feelings, and Sarah did the same. We were able to connect on a level that I never thought was possible. And it was all because we were willing to take a risk and be vulnerable with each other.

Building emotional intimacy and vulnerability wasn't easy, but it was worth it. It allowed us to connect on a deeper level, build trust, and create a relationship that was stronger and more meaningful than either of us ever thought possible.

Chapter 6: Creating shared goals and values in relationships

Creating shared goals and values in relationships is essential for building a strong and healthy partnership. When both individuals in a relationship have a clear understanding of what they want to achieve and what they stand for, it can help to foster trust, communication, and mutual respect.

One of the first steps in creating shared goals and values is to have open and honest conversations about what is important to each person. This can include discussing things like career aspirations, financial goals, and personal values such as honesty, loyalty, and integrity.

It's also important to understand that goals and values may change over time, and to be open to discussing these changes as they happen. For example, a couple may start out with a shared goal of saving money for a down payment on a house, but later, one partner may decide to pursue a different career path that requires a move to another city. In this case, it's important for the couple to discuss how this change in plans may affect their shared goals and come up with a new plan that works for both of them.

Another way to create shared goals and values is by setting specific, measurable, and achievable goals together. For example, a couple may decide to set a goal of saving a certain amount of money for a vacation, and then work together to come up with a budget and a plan for achieving that goal. This can help to build a sense of teamwork and cooperation, and can also provide a sense of accomplishment when the goal is reached.

It's also important to find ways to align your actions with your shared goals and values.

For example, if honesty is a value you both prioritize, make sure to be transparent and truthful in all your interactions. Or if one of your shared goals is to maintain a healthy lifestyle, find ways to support each other in making healthy choices, such as cooking healthy meals together or going on regular walks.

In summary, creating shared goals and values in relationships is essential for building a strong and healthy partnership. It's important to have open and honest conversations about what is important to each person, understand that goals and values may change over time and be open to discussing these changes. Additionally, setting specific and measurable goals together, and aligning actions with shared goals and values can help to build a sense of teamwork and cooperation in the relationship.

Benefits of Creating shared goals and values in relationships

Creating shared goals and values in relationships can lead to several benefits, such as:

- Improved communication: When both partners have a clear understanding of each other's goals and values, it can facilitate more effective and efficient communication.

- Increased trust and intimacy: When partners share goals and values, it can create a sense of trust and intimacy as they are working towards common objectives together.

- Greater sense of shared purpose: Having shared goals and values can give partners a sense of shared purpose, which can help to strengthen the relationship.

- Better decision-making: When partners share goals and values, it can make decision-making easier, as they are likely to be aligned on what is important to them.

- Increased motivation and commitment: When partners share goals and values, it can increase motivation and commitment to work together to achieve those objectives.

How does Creating shared goals and values in relationships influence relationship emotionally

Creating shared goals and values in relationships can have a positive influence on the emotional aspect of the relationship. When partners share goals and values, it can lead to:

- Increased emotional intimacy: When partners are working together towards common goals and values, it can create a deeper sense of emotional intimacy as they share experiences and emotions.

- Greater sense of security and stability: When partners share goals and values, it can create a sense of security and stability in the relationship as they are working towards a shared future.

- Improved emotional support: When partners share goals and values, it can create a stronger sense of emotional support as they are working together to achieve their shared objectives.

- Reduced emotional conflict: When partners share goals and values, it can reduce emotional conflict as they are likely to be aligned on what is important to them.

- Greater emotional satisfaction: When partners share goals and values, it can lead to greater emotional satisfaction as they feel a sense of accomplishment and fulfillment in achieving their shared objectives.

However, it's also important to note that sharing goals and values is not a panacea and it doesn't guarantee a successful relationship. Relationship is complex and multi-faceted and shared goals and values are just one aspect of it. Other factors such as communication, trust, and compatibility are also important.

Chapter 7: Managing expectations and avoiding disappointment

Managing expectations and avoiding disappointment in a relationship is crucial for maintaining a healthy and happy partnership. Having unrealistic expectations of your partner can lead to disappointment and frustration, while setting clear and realistic expectations can help ensure that both parties feel satisfied and fulfilled in the relationship.

One key aspect of managing expectations is being open and honest with your partner about what you want and need from the relationship. This includes communicating your needs and desires, as well as your boundaries and limitations. It's important to be clear about what you can and cannot tolerate in a relationship, and to be open to hearing your partner's needs and boundaries as well.

Another important aspect of managing expectations is being realistic about what your partner can and cannot provide. It's important to remember that no one person can meet all of your needs, and that it's unrealistic to expect your partner to always be able to fulfill your every desire. Instead, try to focus on the things that your partner can offer and appreciate those things.

One way to avoid disappointment in a relationship is to practice forgiveness. It's important to remember that everyone makes mistakes, and that your partner is human and will inevitably fall short at times. Instead of holding onto resentment and anger, try to be understanding and forgiving when your partner makes mistakes.

Another way to avoid disappointment is to set realistic expectations. If you set your expectations too high, you are more likely to be disappointed when your partner doesn't meet them. Instead, try to set expectations that are reasonable and achievable.

In summary, managing expectations and avoiding disappointment in a relationship is essential for maintaining a healthy and happy partnership. This can be achieved by being open and honest with your partner, being realistic about what your partner can and cannot provide, practicing forgiveness, and setting realistic expectations. Remember that it takes time and effort to build and maintain a strong relationship, but it is well worth it in the end.

What impact does Managing expectations and avoiding disappointment have in a relationship?

Managing expectations and avoiding disappointment in a relationship can have a significant impact on the overall health and happiness of the partnership. When expectations are managed effectively, both partners feel satisfied and fulfilled in the relationship, and are less likely to experience disappointment and frustration.

One of the main benefits of managing expectations is that it can help to prevent misunderstandings and conflicts. When expectations are clear and communicated openly, both partners know what to expect and can work together to meet each other's needs. This can lead to a more harmonious and stable relationship.

Managing expectations can also help to foster trust and intimacy in a relationship. When partners feel that their needs and boundaries are respected, they are more likely to feel safe and secure in the relationship, which can lead to deeper emotional connections.

Avoiding disappointment is also important for maintaining a healthy relationship. When disappointment is avoided, partners feel more satisfied with their relationship and are less likely to experience negative emotions such as resentment and anger. This can lead to a more positive and peaceful relationship overall.

In summary, managing expectations and avoiding disappointment in a relationship can have a significant impact on the overall health and happiness of the partnership. It helps to prevent misunderstandings and conflicts, fosters trust and intimacy and leads to more positive and peaceful relationship. By making an effort to manage expectations and avoid disappointment, couples can build a stronger and more fulfilling relationship.

Managing expectations and avoiding disappointment in a relationship is essential for maintaining a healthy and happy partnership. Here is a guide on how to effectively manage expectations and avoid disappointment in your relationship:

Communicate openly and honestly: One of the most important aspects of managing expectations is being open and honest with your partner about what you want and need from the relationship. This includes communicating your needs, desires, boundaries, and limitations. By being open and honest with your partner, you can ensure that both of you are on the same page and that your expectations are clear.

Be realistic: Another important aspect of managing expectations is being realistic about what your partner can and cannot provide. It's important to remember that no one person can meet all of your needs, and that it's unrealistic to expect your partner to always be able to fulfill your every desire. Instead, focus on the things that your partner can offer and appreciate those things.

Practice forgiveness: One way to avoid disappointment in a relationship is to practice forgiveness. Everyone makes mistakes, and it's important to remember that your partner is human and will inevitably fall short at times. Instead of holding onto resentment and anger, try to be understanding and forgiving when your partner makes mistakes.

Set realistic expectations: If you set your expectations too high, you are more likely to be disappointed when your partner doesn't meet them. Instead, try to set expectations that are reasonable and achievable.

Show gratitude: Show gratitude for the things your partner does for you, it will help you appreciate the small things and it will help you to set your expectations accordingly

Take responsibility for your emotions: Your partner is not responsible for your happiness and emotional well-being. Instead, take responsibility for your own emotions and work on developing healthy coping mechanisms.

Be flexible: Be open to change and compromise. Relationship is a dynamic process, and it's normal for things to change over time. Be flexible and open to new ways of doing things to avoid disappointment

Seek help if needed: If you're struggling to manage expectations or avoid disappointment in your relationship, don't hesitate to seek help from a therapist or counselor.

By following this guide, you can effectively manage expectations and avoid disappointment in your relationship. Remember that it takes time and effort to build and maintain a strong relationship, but it is well worth it in the end.

Chapter 8: Maintaining a positive attitude and mindset

Maintaining a positive attitude and mindset in a relationship is crucial for the health and longevity of the partnership. A positive attitude and mindset can help to foster trust, communication, and a sense of emotional safety within the relationship.

One way to maintain a positive attitude and mindset in a relationship is to practice gratitude. This means actively looking for and focusing on the things that you are grateful for in your partner and in your relationship. This can help to shift your focus away from any negative aspects of the relationship and towards the positive aspects.

Another way to maintain a positive attitude and mindset is to practice active listening.

This means truly listening to your partner when they speak and trying to understand their perspective, even if it differs from your own. It also means being open to feedback and willing to work through any issues that may arise in the relationship.

It's also important to communicate openly and honestly with your partner. This means being able to express your thoughts and feelings in a clear and respectful manner, and also being willing to hear your partner's thoughts and feelings, even if they may be difficult to hear.

In addition, it's important to focus on the present moment and not dwell on past mistakes or conflicts. It's natural to have disagreements and conflicts in any relationship, but it's important to learn from them and move forward, rather than dwelling on them and allowing them to negatively impact the present.

Another way to maintain a positive attitude and mindset is to make sure that you are taking care of yourself. This means engaging in activities that bring you joy and fulfillment, such as hobbies, exercise, or spending time with friends and family. It also means making sure that you are getting enough rest and taking care of your physical and emotional well-being.

It's also important to have realistic expectations of your relationship. It's important to remember that relationships take work and that no relationship is perfect. It's also important to remember that people change and grow over time, and that the dynamic of a relationship may change as well.

Finally, it's important to remember that a positive attitude and mindset is a choice. It's easy to fall into the trap of negative thinking and to focus on the negative aspects of a relationship, but it's important to remember that you have the power to choose your thoughts and attitudes.

In conclusion, maintaining a positive attitude and mindset in a relationship is crucial for the health and longevity of the partnership. It requires actively looking for and focusing on the things that you are grateful for, practicing active listening, communicating openly and honestly, focusing on the present moment, taking care of yourself, having realistic expectations and remembering that it's a choice. By incorporating these techniques into your relationship, you can help to foster trust, communication, and emotional safety, ultimately leading to a happier and more fulfilling partnership.

A guide for Maintaining a positive attitude and mindset in a relationship

Maintaining a positive attitude and mindset in a relationship is essential for the overall health and happiness of the partnership. Here are some tips to help you maintain a positive attitude and mindset in your relationship:

- Practice gratitude: Make a conscious effort to focus on the things that you are grateful for in your partner and in your relationship. This can help shift your focus away from any negative aspects of the relationship and towards the positive.

- Practice active listening: Listen to your partner when they speak, try to understand their perspective, and be open to feedback. This can help to foster trust and communication within the relationship.

- Communicate openly and honestly: Express your thoughts and feelings in a clear and respectful manner, and be willing to hear your partner's thoughts and feelings, even if they may be difficult to hear.

- Focus on the present moment: Don't dwell on past mistakes or conflicts. Learn from them and move forward, rather than allowing them to negatively impact the present.

- Take care of yourself: Engage in activities that bring you joy and fulfillment, such as hobbies, exercise, or spending time with friends and family. Make sure you are getting enough rest and taking care of your physical and emotional well-being.

- Have realistic expectations: Remember that relationships take work and that no relationship is perfect. Also, people change and grow over time, and the dynamic of the relationship may change as well.

- Make a choice: Remember that a positive attitude and mindset is a choice. It's easy to fall into the trap of negative thinking, but you have the power to choose your thoughts and attitudes.

By incorporating these tips into your relationship, you can help to foster trust, communication, and emotional safety, ultimately leading to a happier and more fulfilling partnership. Remember, maintaining a positive attitude and mindset in a relationship takes effort and commitment, but it is worth it in the long run.

Benefits of Maintaining a positive attitude and mindset in a relationship

There are many benefits to maintaining a positive attitude and mindset in a relationship. Some of the most significant benefits include:

- Improved communication: A positive attitude and mindset can help to foster open and honest communication, which is crucial for a healthy relationship.

- Increased trust: When partners have a positive attitude and mindset, they are more likely to trust each other, which can lead to a stronger bond.

- Reduced stress and conflict: A positive attitude and mindset can help to reduce stress and conflicts within the relationship, leading to a more peaceful and harmonious partnership.

- Greater emotional intimacy: A positive attitude and mindset can help partners to feel more emotionally connected, leading to a greater sense of intimacy and fulfillment.

- Increased resilience: A positive attitude and mindset can help partners to better cope with challenges and setbacks, leading to a greater sense of resilience.

- Better problem-solving: A positive attitude and mindset can help to foster a more productive approach to problem-solving, leading to more effective solutions and greater satisfaction in the relationship.

- Greater happiness: A positive attitude and mindset can lead to greater happiness and satisfaction in the relationship, which can improve the overall well-being of both partners.

Overall, maintaining a positive attitude and mindset in a relationship can help to create a stronger and more fulfilling partnership, and can lead to greater happiness and well-being for both partners.